WHAT AM I?

Quick, Quiet, and Feathered

WHAT AM I?

By Moira Butterfield
Illustrated by Wayne Ford

RSVP

RAINTREE
STECK-VAUGHN
P U B L I S H E R S
The Steck-Vaughn Company

Austin, Texas

Published by Raintree Steck-Vaughn Publishers, an imprint of Steck-Vaughn Company

Editors: Jilly MacLeod, Kathy DeVico
Project Manager: Joyce Spicer
Electronic Production: Amy Atkinson
Designer: Helen James
Illustrator: Wayne Ford / Wildlife Art Agency

Library of Congress Cataloging-in-Publication Data

Butterfield, Moira, 1961-
    Quick, quiet, and feathered/by Moira Butterfield; illustrated by Wayne Ford.
    p.   cm. — (What am I?)
    Summary: A riddle asking the reader to guess which animal is being described precedes information about different parts of a barn owl's body, how it behaves, and where it lives.
    ISBN 0-8172-4585-5
    1. Barn owl — Juvenile literature.   [1. Barn owl. 2. Owls.] I. Ford, Wayne, ill. II. Title. III. Series.
QL696.S85B88 1997
598.9'7 — dc20   96-30860
                          CIP   AC

Printed in Portugal.
Bound in the United States.
1 2 3 4 5 6 7 8 9 0 LB 99 98 97 96

I have feathers and a beak.
And long sharp talons on my feet.
I hunt at night with shining eyes.
People say I'm very wise.

What am I?

Here is my eye.

My eyes are big and round. They help me see in the dark. I like to hunt at night and sleep during the day.

I sit quietly in the shadows, watching for small animals to run by. I will catch them and eat them, if I can.

Here is my head.

My ears are hidden
under my feathers.
I can hear very well.
I listen for squeaking
and rustling noises.

I can hear something
moving in the grass
below. It had better
watch out. Can
you see what
it is?

Here is my wing.

My wings are very
long. When I see
something to eat,
I spread my wings
and fly very quietly
through the night.

The mouse does not
hear me coming. When
I am overhead, I swoop
down and grab it.
Then I carry it back
to my home.

Here are my talons.

My talons are long,
sharp claws on the
ends of my toes.
I use them to catch
food. I can grip very
tightly with them.

When I sit in a tree,
I curl my talons
tightly around a
branch. I can sleep
for hours sitting
up like this.

Here are my feathers.

I have long, speckled feathers on my back and wings. The feathers on my belly are short, white, and fluffy.

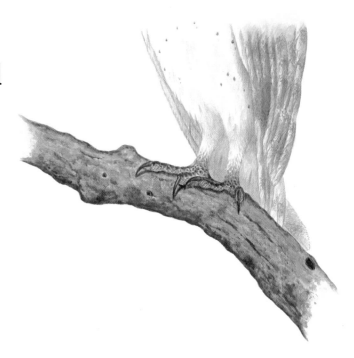

Sometimes I clean my feathers by splashing in a puddle. Then I find a safe place to sit and dry off.

Here is my beak.

I use it to tear my
food into little pieces
small enough for me
to swallow. I only like
to eat meat.

I often eat fur or
bones, but I don't
like them. So I
cough them up
again, squeezed
together in little
balls called pellets.

Here is my home.

It may be inside a hole in a tree or in a quiet building. Sometimes I warn other birds to stay away from my home.

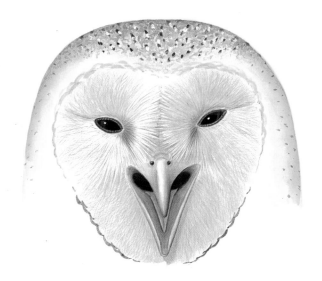

I open my beak and...
screech!
Have you guessed what I am?

I am an owl.

Point to my ...

sharp talons.

round eyes.

pointed beak.

long wings.

white belly.

speckled feathers.

I am called
a barn owl.

21

Here are my babies.

They are called chicks or owlets. At first, they cannot fly. I go hunting and bring them food to eat.

Slowly my owlets grow until they are big enough to fly away. Next year, I will have some more babies.

Here is my territory.

It is
the place
where I live
and hunt for food.

Can you see a mouse, a bat, two frogs, three rabbits, and a beetle?

Here is a map of the world.

I live in lots of different countries. Can you see some of the places where I live?

Can you point to the place where you live?

North America

South America

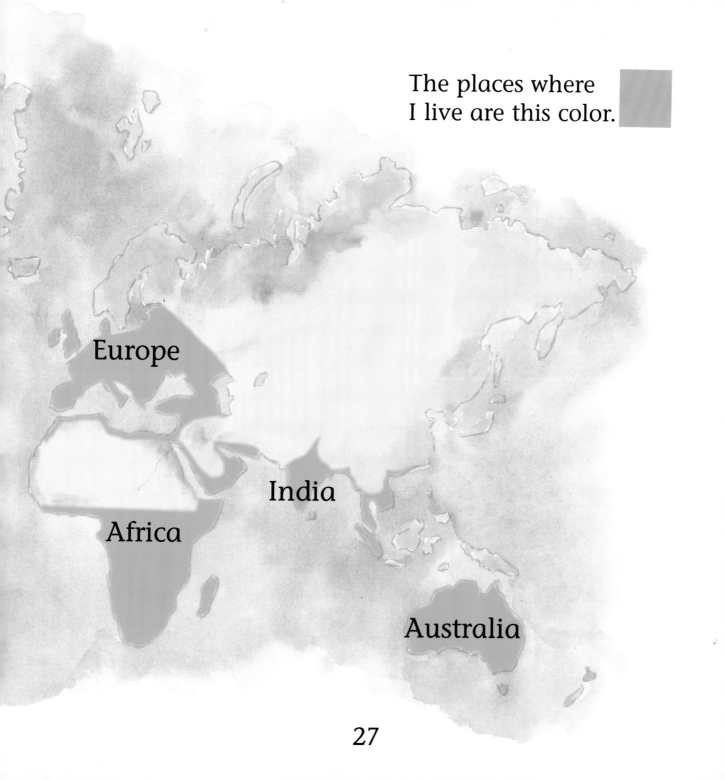

The places where
I live are this color.

Europe

India

Africa

Australia

27

Can you answer these questions about me?

Do I hunt during the day, or in the night?

Can I see in the dark?

What do I like to eat?

What are my claws called?

Do my feathers all look the same?

Do I have any ears?

Where do I make
my home?

What are my babies
called?

Do I sleep lying down?

29

Here are words to help you learn about me.

feather Feathers are made up of lots of tiny soft, fluffy strands. I have some long ones and some short ones.

glide When I stretch my wings wide and float softly along.

owlet The name for one of my babies.

pellet A little rounded ball made up of fur and bones from my last meal. I cough up pellets every day.

plunge When I swoop down very fast.

screech The loud noise I make to warn others to stay away.

speckled Colored with lots of tiny dots, like my wing feathers.

talons My long, sharp claws. I have four on each foot.

territory The place where I live. I often live in grasslands and hunt for food on the edge of woods.